IS GOD FOR REAL?

Believing in the God Who is There

Jeriah D. Shank
Teresa Hemmings

Illustrated by Emma Nichols

Dear Reader,

Have you ever wondered who God really is and if you can truly believe in Him? People ask a lot of questions about believing in God. Where did the Bible come from? Why do so many bad things happen in the world? Did God really create everything? Did Jesus really rise from the dead, and if He did, what difference does that make? These are excellent questions, and we're excited to help you begin answering them!

We'd like you to meet Samantha and Joshua, a sister/brother duo who are learning and growing in their knowledge of God. Ten-year-old Samantha and nine-year-old Joshua have lots of questions, and in this book you'll get to listen in as they talk through some really important things with their dad and mom.

We invite you to follow along with Samantha and Joshua as they learn more about believing and following the God who is there and who wants us to know Him more! Take a few minutes to talk about the questions at the end of each chapter and let what you learn become part of your story too!

Keep asking good questions, young friends!

Jeriah Shank, Teresa Hemmings, and Emma Nichols

From Jeriah:

For my Bean, Bug, and Peanut,

I love you and I hope this book will help you and encourage you to love the Lord your God with all your heart, soul, and mind! Matthew 22:37

From Teresa:

For my HemmKids,

I hope you always remember that the Bible can handle your tough questions, and I pray you always delight in the Way, the Truth, and the Life.

From Emma:

To my parents for teaching me to ask worthwhile questions and always seeking to provide answers.

Is God for Real? Yes, and this book should be in every family's library. As a father of six children and now as a grandfather, I am thrilled to see such a wonderful resource being available. Having now been a pastor for many years, I am convinced that we are waiting too long to begin teaching apologetics (knowing and defending Christian beliefs) to our children. This book is the best place to begin for addressing this urgent need, especially to parents who aren't sure where to begin.

PASTOR JAY LUCAS, Senior Pastor Of Grace Community Church, Washington Courthouse, OH and author of several books, including *Ask Them Why: How To Help Unbelievers Find The Truth.*

Is God for Real? is a charming and lovely introduction into basic Christian apologetics for kids. If you're a mom or dad, and you've tried looking for apologetics books for your littles, then you know how hard it is to find something like this. *Is God for Real?* is a good story, beautifully illustrated, with strong Christian teaching, well-rooted in Scripture, and rarest of all, it surveys a handful of apologetics topics including the reliability of Scripture, arguments for God, Jesus's resurrection, and why God allows evil. Each chapter also has a mini discussion guide with Bible verses, making for a smooth transition from story-time into Bible-study. I have to commend Jeriah Shank and Teresa Hemmings for this helpful little book. I trust many homes will be blessed by it.

DR. JOHN D. FERRER, Equal Rights Institute and CrossExamined Ministries.

If you are a Sunday school teacher/educator/mother, *Is God for Real?* should be in your library! As an educator, when my students are preparing to read a new story, I ask them to make "connections" as they read. How does the text connect to self? How does the text connect to other text you have read? How does the text relate to the world? *Is God for Real?* is full of these types of connections which make the book impactful in different ways to different readers. Personal connections when reading are so important and I feel that anyone who picks up this book will be able to take away truly meaningful aspects of God's Word that relate to their existence.

DARCI ROORDA, Mom, Educator.

Have you ever wanted to help your children or grandchildren understand and defend their faith? This beautifully illustrated book will be a great resource to read with them. *Is God for Real?* reads like a storybook, yet introduces hard concepts without being too wordy or too simplistic. Discussions of origins, sin, the nature of God and other topics are brought up naturally and questions at the end of the chapters aid in discussing them. What a wonderful addition this book will be to the family library.

JEANNIE VOGEL, Bible Study author and Women's Ministry Consultant and Nana to seven.

Jeriah and Teresa, with the help of some beautiful illustrations from Emma, help answer nine of the basic questions that many children have. The format is accessible, the Scripture is taught, and room is left for further discussion. What more could you want?

DAVID ROBERTSON, Well–known pastor and apologist.

Is God for Real? is a valuable book for young people trying to make sense of their Christian faith. It's too easy to sleepwalk through Sunday school, going for the fellowship and food and forgetting the Christian instruction that is able to save our souls (1 Timothy 4:16). The most important questions we can ask are the ones that challenge our faith. This book asks those questions and sketches biblically orthodox answers, with suggested further readings to provide still fuller answers. I highly recommend this book.

DR. BILL DEMBSKI, Author of many books on Intelligent Design.

Scripture quotations taken from The Holy Bible, New International Version® NIV®Copyright © 1973, 1978, 1984, 2011 by Biblica, Inc. TM used by permission. All rights reserved worldwide.

Cover design by Catriona Mackenzie

Printed and bound by Gutenberg, Malta

Contents

I. WHO IS GOD?

"Samantha, Joshua! Time to go," called Mom out of the open window in their family car.

"Coming!" replied Samantha. She quickly hugged Mrs. Nelson, her favorite Sunday School teacher, and waved goodbye to her friend, Ryleigh. "See you next week!"

"Race you!" Joshua challenged as he darted towards the car and scrambled into his seat. His seat belt clicked at the same time as Samantha's door opened.

Hopping into her seat, Samantha pulled the seat belt across her body, but as she started to buckle it, her Bible fell off her lap, dropping open on the floor and spilling out her Sunday School papers.

"Here, I'll get those," offered Mom, reaching back and picking up the mess.

"What a great day at church! Samantha, what did you learn about in Sunday School today?" Dad asked as he checked his mirror and started backing out of the parking space.

"We had a really interesting lesson! Mrs. Nelson taught us what God is like!"

"Oh yeah?" asked Dad. "What is God like?"

"Well," responded Samantha, "she said God knows everything, can do anything He wants to, and, um . . . oh yeah, He is everywhere.

"We read a lot from some psalm, but I don't really remember now what it said," Joshua added.

Mom looked at one of the papers she had picked up. "Was it Psalm 139? It's right here on your Sunday School paper. Should I read it?"

"Yeah! There was some really cool stuff in there!" declared Samantha.

"*O LORD, you have searched me and you know me. You know when I sit and when I rise; you perceive my thoughts from afar. You discern my going out and my lying down; you are familiar with all my ways. Before a word is on my tongue, you know it completely, O LORD. You hem me in – behind and before; you have laid your hand upon me. Such knowledge is too wonderful for me, too lofty for me to attain. Where can I go from your Spirit? Where can I flee from your presence? If I go up to the heavens, you are there; if I make my bed in the depths, you are there. If I rise on the wings of the dawn, if I settle on the far side of the sea, even there your hand will guide me, your right hand will hold me fast* (Psalm 139:1-10)."

"Wow!" said Dad. "God is awesome!"

"We also learned that God has always existed and that He isn't made up of stuff like we are," Joshua interjected.

"I just read a verse recently that talks about that," added Dad. "It was I Timothy 1:17, and it calls God eternal, immortal, and invisible. Just like you were saying, He has existed forever and isn't made up of matter, like us. We call that 'immaterial.' It means He doesn't have a physical body, and so we can't see God like we see each other."

"That sounds like quite a Sunday School lesson!" exclaimed Mom.

"That wasn't even all! Mrs. Nelson also told us that God is perfect and never does anything wrong. But He still loves us even when we do wrong things," said Samantha.

"So true!" said Mom. "Look up Psalm 36:5 and 6 when we get home. It says exactly what you just said."

"So, Samantha and Joshua, if God is so amazing, what does that mean for us?" asked Dad.

"I don't know," responded Joshua. "I'm really glad that God knows about everything and that He can be everywhere all at once."

"I'm also kind of glad He's not just like us," added Samantha, "because it would be weird if God could get hurt and die like we do. I noticed that a couple of the songs we sang in church talked about who God is, and I felt like I was really worshipping God when I sang along."

"You got it, kiddo. When we know who God is, we can worship Him better and it helps us obey Him more willingly, too. The good news is that God gave us His Word so that we can know about Him. God isn't just a super powered human being, as if He is just like us but better. As the Creator of all, though there are ways He is similar to us,

He is still very different. Even our words do not fully capture who He is. But He tells us what He is like so we can know Him and His love for us and so we can love Him, too! Keep reading, and you'll learn lots and lots of truths about who God is."

"Well, I do have a question. Mrs. Nelson also said something about how God is trina … trini …" Samantha stumbled.

"Trinity?" supplied Mom.

"Yeah! Trinity. What does that mean?" asked Samantha.

"Good question," answered Dad, "but here we are at home, and it's time for lunch. How about we tackle this question later today?"

"Sounds good!" Samantha responded while Joshua unbuckled and darted out of the car.

"Someone must be hungry," chuckled Dad as the rest of the family followed the smell of lunch into the house.

Scripture to Read: Psalm 100

Verse to Memorize: Psalm 100:5

Discussion Questions:

1. Why should we try to learn about God?

2. What are three things you know to be true about God?

3. How can we know what God is like?

4. How can you grow to know God better?

2. WHAT IS THE TRINITY?

Samantha had just snuggled under her soft comforter and found the just-right spot in her pillow when Dad peeked in her half-closed door.

"All settled in here, Samantha?" he asked as he switched off the overhead light. Samantha's nightlight softly illuminated the dark corners of her room.

"Yep!" Samantha answered. "But Daddy, remember you said we could talk about what 'Trinity' means tonight?"

"Oh yeah! I forgot already. Are you sure you shouldn't be sleeping?"

"I promise I'll go to sleep right away when you leave, but will you tell me what it means that God is a Trinity first?"

Dad came into her room and sat on the end of her bed. "Alright, if you promise to go right to sleep after. Do you have your Bible handy?"

Samantha sat up, grabbed her Bible off her nightstand, and flipped on the reading light. "Got it!"

"Look up Deuteronomy 6:4 and read it to me."

Samantha flipped through the pages at the beginning of her Bible. "It says, 'Hear, O Israel: The LORD our God, the LORD is one.'"

"So, according to that verse, how many gods are there?" Dad questioned.

"It says there is just one."

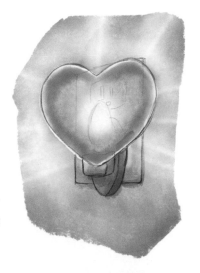

"That's right. The whole Bible clearly says that there's only one God and He is the only Being worthy of worship. But while there is only one God, the Bible also calls three Persons 'God.' 'Trinity' is a word that we use to describe how our one God is also three Persons."

"Yeah, yeah! Mrs. Nelson said that."

"Mrs. Nelson said what?" asked a quiet voice from the hallway.

"Joshua, what are you doing out of bed?" Dad questioned.

Joshua crept into Samantha's room. "I heard you two talking through the wall, and I wanted to know what you were talking about."

"Well, I guess since you were in on the conversation earlier today, you may as well stay for a minute or two." Dad patted the bed beside him, and Joshua quickly hopped on.

"We were talking about how God is one God, but He is also described as 'Trinity'," Dad continued.

"The Father, the Son, and the Holy Spirit, right?" Samantha inserted.

"Right! In Matthew 28:19, Jesus says, 'Therefore go and make disciples of all nations, baptizing them in the name of the Father and of the Son and of the Holy Spirit.' The concept of the Trinity is that within one God there are three Persons who are equal and eternal, but are also distinct. Do you know what 'distinct' means?"

"Umm . . . no," replied Samantha as Joshua shook his head.

"'Distinct' means that you can tell them apart. The Father is not the Son or the Spirit, the Son is not the Father or the Spirit, and the Spirit is not the Father or the Son. Each Person has His own name and relation to the others and, throughout the Bible, we see them doing things. But while we can tell them apart, they are not parts of God or three gods that happen to get along really well, but one God and so each Person equally shares one nature, one will, and one purpose. So when we sing and pray to God, we are really speaking of all three Persons at once!"

"I'm not sure I get it, Daddy," mumbled Joshua.

Dad chuckled. "That puts you in good company, Joshua! No one completely understands the Trinity because we can't quite wrap our human brains around everything God reveals about Himself. But we know it's true because the Bible tells us over and over again that it's true. Do you remember when Jesus was baptized by John the Baptist?"

"I do!" exclaimed Samantha. "Well, kind of."

"Here, can I borrow your Bible?" Dad reached for Samantha's Bible and flipped to the middle. "Matthew 3:16 and 17 say, 'As soon as Jesus was baptized, he went up out of the water. At that moment heaven was opened, and he saw the Spirit of God descending like a dove and alighting on him. And a voice from heaven said, "This is my Son, whom I love; with him I am well pleased."' Here, we see the Son, who is named, 'Jesus,' the Spirit, and the Father all at the same

time. This is only one of many places in the Bible where we see the three Persons of the Trinity interacting in their own distinct ways. The Father sent the Son to the world and the Spirit is sent by the Father and the Son. But how many gods are there?"

"Just one," Samantha affirmed.

"We can't fully understand God, because, like we talked about this morning, He's immaterial and not limited by space and bodies like we are and He isn't limited by our mental abilities either. People throughout history have tried to illustrate the Trinity by comparing it to things we can understand, but no illustration really compares to God, who is so much greater than us and created us. But it's okay that we don't completely get it. It's great news that our one God is so far beyond anything we can imagine! God is the only one who is completely like God. That's why He's so worthy of our love, praise, and obedience," added Dad.

The room was quiet for a moment as Samantha and Joshua both thought about what their dad had just said. Dad closed Samantha's Bible and put it back on the nightstand.

"I guess that makes sense, Daddy," said Samantha, "but how do I know this is all real?"

"Yeah! Why do we believe that God is real if we can't see Him or understand everything about Him?" Joshua asked.

"These are really great questions, but we're all going to be in trouble if you two don't get to sleep soon. How about we tackle that subject tomorrow? Joshua, it's time for you to get back to your room."

"Okay, Daddy. G'night." Joshua gave his dad a quick hug and then slipped out of the room.

Dad turned off Samantha's reading light and kissed her forehead. "Sleep tight, Samantha."

"Night, Daddy," Samantha murmured drowsily as her eyelids drifted shut.

Scripture To Read: Matthew 28:18-20

Verse To Memorize: Matthew 28:19

Discussion Questions:

1. Summarize the idea of the Trinity in your own words.

2. If all three Persons of the Trinity are God, are they all equal? Can any of them be more "God" than the others?

3. Do you have to understand everything about God in order to believe in Him? Why or why not?

4. What do the names, "Father," "Son," and "Holy Spirit" tell us about what God is like?

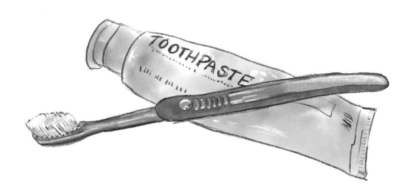

3. DOES GOD EXIST?

"Earth to Joshua!" called Mom. Joshua jumped and quickly pulled his plate away from the trash can, where he was about to throw it away.

As he placed his plate and silverware on the counter by the sink instead, Dad asked, "Is there something wrong, buddy? You seemed kind of out of it during supper."

Joshua sighed as his head drooped low. "I had a really bad day at school today. My teacher was really grumpy, and then I found out that Ellie gets to compete in the state art competition. I thought I would get to. To make it worse, Ben wouldn't talk to me at recess. He only wants to play with his basketball teammates now."

"Oh man, I'm sorry you had a rough day," Mom said as she wrapped an arm around Joshua's shoulders and guided him into the living room. Settling on the couch with Joshua pulled close, she continued, "Bad days can be so hard, but those are the days I'm especially thankful that God is always with me."

Joshua pulled away from his mom. "That's the thing, though! How do I really know that God is for real? I can't see Him or get hugs from Him like I do from you. Some of my classmates make fun of me and say that I can't prove God exists, and I didn't know how to answer them. Sometimes," Joshua paused, "sometimes I even think they might be right."

Dad carried his mug into the living room and settled into the chair beside the couch. "These are really good questions, Joshua. We were

kind of talking about this last night, weren't we?" He took a slurp of his steaming coffee and grimaced. "There are lots of things we know without seeing them. For instance, my tongue just got burned and it hurts. I know pain exists, but I can't see it. You know hurt feelings exist, even though you can't see them, right?"

"Yeah, I guess," answered Joshua, "but I don't know what that has to do with proving that God exists."

"Well," continued his dad, "first off, we believe that God exists because He told us He does. Hebrews 11:6 says that without faith, it is impossible to please God and that if we want to know Him we have to believe He exists. But our faith is not blind. In other words, we don't believe without evidence. There are lots of good reasons to believe that God is real."

"Like what?" asked Joshua.

"Do you remember what the very first verse of the Bible, Genesis 1:1, says?" quizzed Dad.

"'In the beginning, God created the heavens and the earth,'" Joshua answered.

"Right! When we look at our world and the universe around us, it's clear that it all came from somewhere. Getting something from nothing is called magic! Nothing can't make anything. Everything that has a beginning was made by something or someone else. For instance, our supper tonight did not just appear. It must have come from somewhere, and someone or something must have made it. Thanks for a great supper, by the way, Mom."

"You're certainly welcome," she chimed in. "And you know, that brings up another point about creation pointing to God's existence. Our spaghetti, peas, and garlic bread were made on purpose. They weren't just thrown together by chance. I know how to make those things, and I created them. Some people say that all we see around us happened by chance over billions of years, but the amazing amount of detail and design we see in things like leaves, bugs, and the human body tell us that we have an intelligent Creator."

Joshua picked up a fidget toy from the couch and started twirling it in his hands. "Okay, so God designed everything in creation on purpose. But who created God? And how did He know how to create everything?"

"Wow, Joshua! Those are some deep questions. I love them!" exclaimed Dad. "Remember what you learned in Sunday School about God being eternal and immaterial? Everything that is made of matter and stuff wears out. That's why Mom has to keep buying you new clothes! The whole universe is also slowly wearing out. But since God isn't made of stuff, He didn't need a creator. If He did, then we would have to ask what created Him and what created that creator, and on and on forever. For anything to begin, there must be something that didn't have a beginning. God is eternal and never began … and He'll never end! As God, He is also complete in knowledge and wisdom. Here, let me show you something."

Dad grabbed his Bible from the bookshelf beside him and opened it. "Isaiah 40:28 says, 'Do you not know? Have you not heard? The Lord is the everlasting God, the Creator of the ends of the earth. He will not grow tired or weary, and his understanding no one can fathom.'"

"Another way we know God is real is the fact that people know right from wrong," added Mom. She pointed to the toy in Joshua's

hands. "If you decided right now to throw your sister's favorite fidget toy in the trash to be taken away tomorrow when the garbage truck comes, would that be right or wrong?"

"Wait up! That would be wrong! And so mean!"

exclaimed Samantha, running out of the kitchen with dishwater dripping from her hands.

"You're right, Samantha. Everyone knows that stealing someone else's toy and destroying it is wrong," said Mom.

Samantha wiped her hands on her pants and grabbed her toy from Joshua's hands before plopping next to him on the couch.

Mom continued, "But the only way that things can be right or wrong is if we have an ultimate standard, like a measuring stick of right and wrong, to compare with our actions and attitudes. Our measuring stick is the character of God. So, for instance, because God is good and loving, it is right to be good and loving toward others. Without God, things like throwing out Samantha's toys, or even worse things like hurting other people, might still not be nice, but they wouldn't be wrong, just like cutting ahead in line isn't nice, but it isn't illegal either. Think of it this way: Who makes rules for you about when to go to bed?"

"You and Daddy do, of course," answered Joshua.

"The fact that there are rules in our house shows that someone is there to make them. Rules come from people, not nature. There are rules for right and wrong in our world, and, for the most part, people know what those rules are. God, as the Creator of this world, made rules that line up with His character and has put those rules in our hearts and in His Word for us to know. Loving others and helping others is good and right. Hurting others is wrong even if we want to hurt others to make ourselves feel better and even if our culture says it is okay to hurt them. This is a strong reason to believe that God exists," explained Mom.

"I have another one to add as well, and it is a big one!" inserted Dad. "Samantha, remember how we talked about God being a Trinity last night?"

"Sure. The Father, the Son, and the Holy Spirit," answered Samantha.

"Right. Well, the Son, Jesus, was God on earth. He was able to be seen and heard and touched. He claimed to be God and people were ready to kill Him for saying so. But He backed up His words with miracles like giving the blind back their sight, healing sick people, and even bringing people back from the dead. The most powerful proof that He is God is that He rose from the grave three days after He died. Only God can do things like that!"

"So, I guess there are lots of reasons to have faith that God exists, huh?" said Joshua.

"Actually, when you think about it," pondered Samantha, "it's almost harder to believe He doesn't exist."

"Well, you two, both of you need to keep praying for your friends and think about the things we've talked about, and you'll have a good answer to give your friends when they say you can't prove God exists. In the meantime, though, you can be confident yourself that God does exist and that He is with you on your best and your worst days. Just like He's going to be with you while you go finish up your math

homework, right?" Dad winked and playfully pulled Joshua up off the couch.

"And you, Miss Samantha, still have some dishes to dry," called Mom as she led the way back to the kitchen.

Scripture to Read: Psalm 19

Verse to Memorize: Psalm 19:1

Discussion Questions:

1. What are three reasons to believe that God exists?

2. Which of these reasons makes the most sense to you?

3. Which of these reasons seems like the easiest to use when someone claims that you can't prove God's existence?

4. How can knowing that God is real change how we think, feel, and act?

4. HOW DID WE GET THE BIBLE?

"Bills, bills, bills! Why doesn't anyone send friendly letters anymore?" muttered Dad as he sorted through the day's mail stacked on the kitchen table.

Joshua looked up from doodling comic book characters in his sketch book. "We're working on writing letters in school this month. Our teacher found a class in China for us to be pen pals with. We each have to write a letter about ourselves and our family."

"I had a pen pal in school, too," replied Dad. "Mine was from Peru and I learned a lot about what kinds of food he liked and what he did for fun. Having a pen pal is a really neat way to learn firsthand about different cultures. You'll have to tell us about yours when you get a letter."

"You know," began Mom from the other end of the table, where she was reading her book for her women's Bible study, "I was thinking after our talk the other day about how we know that God is real that we didn't really talk about how to learn for yourself about God."

"What do you mean, Mommy?" asked Joshua.

"Like a letter from someone in China is going to tell you a bit about who they are, God's letter tells you what He wants you to know about Him."

"What? God wrote a letter to me?"

"He sure did," chuckled Mom. "In fact, I'm reading it right now." She tapped her pen on her open Bible.

"Oh. You mean the Bible." Joshua's enthusiasm wilted.

"Don't sound so disappointed, Joshua," Dad chimed in. "God worked in some pretty amazing ways to make sure you could read His letter to you."

"Really?"

"Absolutely! Second Timothy 3:16 says, 'All Scripture is God-breathed.' People wrote the Bible—lots of different people, in fact—but God guided them so that they would write exactly what we need to know about Him, about His works, and about how He wants us to live. Second Peter 1:21 teaches, 'But prophets, though human, spoke from God as they were carried along by the Holy Spirit.' The Bible was written over the course of almost 1,600 years by around forty different authors, all so that you and I could know God," said Dad.

"Is that why there are different books inside the Bible?" asked Joshua.

"It is. Different authors wrote different books. For example, Moses, the first leader of Israel in the Old Testament, wrote most of the first five books of the Bible around 1500 B.C. The Gospels, which are the first four books of the New Testament, were written by four of Jesus' close followers and were written after His death and resurrection.

There are letters, poems, books of history, and books that tell about the future. Each of the sixty-six books that make up the Old and New Testament has its own themes, but they all have one purpose: to show us who God is and what His plan is for the ages."

Joshua wrote some numbers on his sketch pad. "So, if the first books of the Bible were written around 1500 B.C., they're, like, 3,500 years old? How do we even still have them?"

"That's part of what Dad was saying about how God has worked so that you can read His letter to you," answered Mom. "The original writings of the Bible were written in different languages, like Hebrew and Greek. They were written on all kinds of pressed grass, called 'papyri,' animal skins, and scrolls. We call these writings 'manuscripts.' But these manuscripts would disintegrate and fade over time so people made copies of them by hand. Lots of copies! Eventually, all the books God wanted us to have were put together in one book, which has been copied and translated into many different languages, including English and Chinese!"

"Couldn't the Bible have been changed with all that copying?" questioned Joshua.

"There are people who would use that question to say we can't trust the Bible," answered Dad. "But archaeologists have found thousands of these manuscripts all over the land of Israel, and even in Europe and Africa. If someone wanted to intentionally change what the Bible said, that would be like trying to change the front-page story in a newspaper after it had been printed and delivered all over the country. You couldn't get away with changing a couple of copies because people would have copies older than yours to see what you have changed! The more copies that archaeologists find of Bible books, the more we see that any changes that have happened were mostly things like spelling errors and differences in the order of words. Even when some of the copies had missing sections or differences that made it hard to understand what the writer was saying, none of the core teachings

of the Bible were affected by these things. Does that make sense?"

"Sure. But at school, Alex told me his dad said the Bible contradicts itself. He said the Bible says one thing in one place and something different in another, so he won't believe it."

"Ah, yes. This is a common objection," affirmed Dad. "That's a big topic, and even some of the smartest people don't have it all figured out, but we know that God's Word is without error, because He cannot lie or be wrong or contradict Himself. A lot of these supposed contradictions can be explained by understanding the background of books and who wrote them. People can write about things differently without denying what others have said. For example, if I asked you and three other people in your class to write a report about your field trip to the science center last week, would your reports be exactly the same?"

"No. We split into different groups, and each group got to pick four different things to do."

"Exactly! Some very common 'contradictions,'" Dad said, using air quotes, "are found in the Gospels, the four books written about Jesus' life. But the four authors were all very different and had different experiences with Jesus and different purposes for writing, so they had different details. Those aren't contradictions, they're just differences."

Just then, Dad's phone started buzzing. "Sorry bud, I have to take this. Good talk, Joshua!"

As Dad left the room, Joshua looked over to his mom reading her Bible study. She glanced up and smiled. "Joshua, I love that you have so many important questions and that you ask us, but I also want you to know that the true way to know God is to read His letter to you for yourself. That way you know if what people say to you is true or not. God has preserved an amazing story of His love for you and His way for you to spend eternity in heaven with Him. Letters from China are great, but letters from God are priceless."

Scripture to Read: 2 Timothy 3:14–17

Verses to Memorize: 2 Timothy 3:16–17

Discussion Questions:

1. What does it mean that the Bible is God's Word?

2. How did we get the Bible we have today?

3. Why can we trust the Bible?

4. Why should we read the Bible?

5. DID GOD REALLY CREATE EVERYTHING?

"Whew!" Samantha puffed as she plopped down beside her dad at the park table and took a long drink from her water bottle. "Joshua wore me out with all that tag! He's still going though." Samantha pointed toward her brother pumping his legs to see how high he could swing.

"He sure does have a lot of energy!" responded Dad. "So how was school today?"

"It was okay. We had an assembly about healthy eating. It was kind of boring and the speaker talked a lot about vegetables, but she gave us all these cool new water bottles," Samantha said, taking another sip.

"Hey, I've been meaning to ask you how your science class is going. I know you have been studying a lot about animals this month. Is that pretty interesting?" asked Dad.

"It really is! Animals are so amazing! Last week we watched a video about Arctic animals. Arctic foxes are so cute!" gushed Samantha. "But today was a little confusing . . ." she trailed off.

"How so?"

"Mr. Stevens showed us a chart in our books that had drawings of the bones in the arms of a few different animals. It showed that the bones in the arms of a human are similar to the fins of a whale and the wings of a bat. He said this shows that we all have a common ancestor that we have evolved from. But I thought that God created everything. It's really confusing, but I didn't want to say anything in class about it."

"I'm so glad that you caught that difference. Evolution is a hard subject to tackle. A lot of people believe it so completely that they aren't willing to think any other way about how we came to be, but whenever anyone talks about how the world began, they're starting with beliefs they assume to be true."

"Mr. Stevens seems pretty sure he knows how the world began," interrupted Samantha.

"I'm sure he does," answered Dad. "But the truth is that no human was around to see how the world started, so every theory about the beginning of the world is actually an issue of faith. Those who believe we all came about by only natural processes, without God, believe that all living creatures we see today started with simple organisms which evolved and changed over billions of years to form all the variety we see today, without direction, purpose, or design. When they see a chart like the one you mentioned, they say, 'Yes! This proves that all creatures came from earlier, different kinds of life forms!' But what do we believe about the beginning of the world, Samantha?" asked her dad.

"That God created the world and everything in it," Joshua panted as he collapsed on the bench next to Dad and started guzzling from his new water bottle.

"Right. And where do we get our belief?"

"From the Bible," both siblings answered.

"Exactly," Dad affirmed. "We believe the Bible's account of creation because it was given to us by the only one who was there: God."

"I believe that, too, but doesn't that chart prove that we all came from common ancestors?" asked Samantha.

"Let's see . . . Picture in your mind the houses on our block. What do they look like?" questioned Dad.

"They're pretty much all the same except they are different colors and some are bigger than others," she answered.

"Did you know that if you went inside our neighbors' houses, you would find a bedroom in the same spot as yours and that the bathrooms and kitchen are all in the same spots as ours too? Why do you think that is?"

"I don't know," shrugged Samantha.

"It's because all the houses on our street have the same designer. He made them all just a little different, but they have lots of similarities. They are made with many of the same materials since houses need bricks, wood, and cement to stand, but they also have differences, like paint, sizes of garages, or number of rooms. That's a very simple way to think about what that chart is actually showing. It's not that all those animals evolved from other kinds of animals. It's showing that all those creatures have the same Designer and were made for similar actions, which is exactly what we read in Genesis," concluded Dad. He picked up his phone, pulled up his Bible app, and navigated to Genesis 1:24. Handing the phone to Samantha, he said, "Here, read this verse."

"And God said, 'Let the land produce living creatures according to their kinds: the livestock, the creatures that move along the ground, and the wild animals, each according to its kind.' And it was so," Samantha read.

"When God created all animals and Adam and Eve, He made them to reproduce according to their kind. Do you know what that means?" When Samantha shook her head no, Dad continued, "If that dog on that leash over there had babies, what kind of babies would they be?"

"Puppies," Samantha answered.

"Right! 'Kinds' are family groups of animals. Dogs make dogs. Cats make cats. Humans make humans. There can be great variety within family groups, and members of those family groups adapt to their surroundings, which is why wolves, German shepherds, and poodles look different, but they are all dogs and will only reproduce other dogs. No matter how many generations we see of dogs, bacteria, birds, cats, or humans, we only see them give birth to their same kind," explained Dad.

"But how do we know that we're right and those others are wrong? If no one was there, how do we really know God created it all?" Joshua challenged.

"That's a really great question, Joshua. Like I said earlier, it's a matter of faith: Will we take God's Word, which comes from Him, or will we ignore what He says and create our own stories? However, just like when we talked about there being good reasons to have faith in

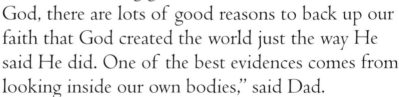

God, there are lots of good reasons to back up our faith that God created the world just the way He said He did. One of the best evidences comes from looking inside our own bodies," said Dad.

"What do you mean by that?" Joshua asked with a puzzled look.

"I mean that if you think about those charts on the wall in the doctor's office, you can see the amazing organs that are at work inside our bodies," he answered.

"Like our lungs and our heart and our stomach," supplied Joshua.

"Exactly! Our body parts are designed to work together to support life. We have brains to think, hearts to pump blood, lungs to receive and use oxygen, stomachs to digest food, and muscles to move our bodies. And it's not just our bodies; the entire world is built with living systems that show purpose to support life, down to your smallest cells and even beyond."

"I get that," inserted Samantha, "but how is that evidence that God created the world?"

"Those who believe in only natural processes believe that, without God, all life began with single celled-organisms which developed piece by piece as creatures gave birth and died off," answered Dad. "They believe that all life forms we know today came about through changes in our genes and trial and error over time, randomly and without any design or purpose. But while random processes can change things, they don't do things with goals in mind. There's no purpose for an end result."

"Oh! But God made all creation with a purpose, right?" concluded Samantha.

"Yes! The Bible says in Psalm 139:14 that we are fearfully and wonderfully made and that God designed the basics of living things so that they would be able to live and enjoy His creation!" exclaimed Dad.

"One other thing that convinces me that God created us is the instruction manual He left inside us," Dad continued

"What instruction manual? Do I have to read it?" groaned Joshua.

"No," Dad chuckled, "but every second, your body is reading it! It's called DNA. DNA contains the instructions in the cells of your body that tell your body parts how to grow, how tall to make you, what color of hair you have, whether you are a boy or girl, and even what you look like."

"But how does that prove that God made us?" Joshua asked.

Turning to Samantha, Dad said, "Samantha, do you remember when we put Joshua's bookshelf together? How did we know how to do that?"

"I remember that! It was fun! I read the instructions to you and you had to do everything I said," laughed Samantha.

"That's right!" said Dad. "We read the instructions and built it. But why did we think the instructions were correct?"

Samantha thought for a moment and answered, "Because the people who made the shelf wrote them."

"Bingo!" said Dad. "Instructions and information only come from minds that can think, plan, and design. If the instructions were made by pets stomping on crayons and smashing them onto paper, we wouldn't expect the instructions to tell us anything.

Joshua giggled and jumped up from the table, stomping his feet and yelling, "I'm an elephant, and I'll stomp on you!" as he moved off toward the playground again. Dad and Samantha laughed at Joshua's antics.

"Because we have information and instructions built into every aspect of us, we know that we are made by a Creator," concluded Dad.

"So, my instructions came from my Creator too. Wow . . ." Samantha marveled.

"Yeah, 'Wow!' God's creation is amazing! Creation clearly shows us God's existence and power. It's sad that so many people reject God's Word and search for all sorts of different answers about how we came to be here."

Dad looked Samantha in the eye, "You know, this is going to be a subject you'll come across so many times in your life. People will want to use science to argue with you and try to make you feel bad because of what you believe. Science is a wonderful tool to understand how the world around us works, but the only reason we can do science is because God made us to understand and care for the world around us. That is why so many of the greatest scientific minds of the past were Christians! Your job is to tell others what you believe and remind them how amazingly they've been made by an intelligent Designer. For now, though, we need to head home. Why don't you grab your fancy new water bottle while I grab your sweaty brother, and we'll get out of here?"

Scripture to Read: Genesis I

Verse to Memorize: Genesis 1:27

Discussion Questions:

1. What assumptions, or beliefs, do naturalists begin with? What assumptions do creationists have?

2. Why do we find similarities between kinds of creation (like humans, horses, apes, and birds)?

3. If God has created everything, who gets to decide the purpose of everything?

4. How could you use the design of your own body to explain to someone that God created everything?

6. DID JESUS RISE FROM THE DEAD?

"Hey! What did you do that for?" cried Joshua, spitting toothpaste on the bathroom mirror as he scolded Samantha.

"It's Easter Sunday, and we're supposed to look our very best," answered Samantha calmly as she patted down the section of Joshua's hair she had just squirted with a spray bottle. "Your hair's sticking up in the back."

"What makes this Sunday any different from last Sunday? Last Sunday I didn't have to wear a dress shirt, and my hair was sticking up then!"

"Don't you remember what Mrs. Nelson taught us about Easter?" asked Samantha?

Joshua rinsed the toothpaste out of his mouth before he answered. "Umm, something about Jesus being better than chocolate?"

Samantha giggled. "Kinda. She said chocolate eggs are fun and all, but the real reason we celebrate Easter is Jesus' resurrection."

"Right! Jesus' rerrusection!" exclaimed Joshua.

"No. Re-sur-rection. When Jesus rose from the grave on the third day after he was crucified on the cross," reminded Samantha.

"I don't like it that Jesus died," said Joshua softly.

"I know, but that's why today is such a big celebration. He didn't stay dead!"

"That's right, Samantha," added Mom, peeking into the bathroom. She leaned against the doorway and asked, "Do you know why it's so important that Jesus rose from the grave?"

"Because it makes everybody happy?" suggested Samantha.

"It does do that, but it's actually way more important than that," her mom explained. "In I Corinthians 15:19, the Bible says that if Jesus didn't rise from the dead, our faith wouldn't mean anything, because Jesus would be just another teacher. When He kept His promise and rose from the dead, He proved that He is God and that He had conquered sin and death for anyone who would believe in Him."

"It seems like everyone would just believe in Him, then, wouldn't they?" Samantha wondered.

"It does seem like that should be the case, but it isn't. Three days after Jesus died, some of His friends returned to His grave and found it open and empty. They told everyone what they saw, but the people who killed Jesus just accused them of stealing His body."

"Did they steal His body?" asked Joshua.

"No they did not, even though some people still think so today. Actually, the fact that they accused the disciples of stealing the body means the tomb was, in fact, empty. Further, the tomb was guarded by Roman soldiers and sealed with a heavy stone. None of Jesus' followers would have been able to overcome the trained soldiers and roll it away. But even if they could, what came next proves even more that Jesus did indeed rise from the dead."

"What happened?" exclaimed Joshua.

"Tell you what," Mom said as she held out Samantha's freshly ironed dress, "Samantha, you get dressed and ready to go. Joshua, you wipe your toothpaste splatters off the mirror. We'll talk more about it on the way to church. We don't want to be late!"

Twenty minutes later, when Samantha and Joshua were dressed in their Easter-best and buckled into the car, Joshua persisted. "So, what happened after Jesus rose from the dead?"

"Well, I Corinthians 15 tells us that He appeared to lots of people," Mom continued. "He showed Himself to Peter and twelve of his closest friends, and then to more than 500 people at one time. He also appeared to His brother, and to Paul, who wrote 1 Corinthians, where we read about the importance of Jesus' resurrection. The interesting part of this, though, is that many of these people were attacked and even killed by the people who didn't believe what they were saying."

"Why is that interesting?" pressed Samantha.

"Let me ask you this: If you made up a story about seeing magical unicorns eating all the plants in our garden, but I told you that if you didn't come clean you would be grounded for a year, what would you do?" asked Mom.

"I would totally tell you the truth! I don't want to be grounded for something that I just made up!" proclaimed Samantha.

"That's right. But these people were willing to suffer and were even killed because they wouldn't admit to lying. I think that's a pretty strong reason to believe they weren't lying in the first place," explained Mom.

"On top of that," inserted Dad, "there were writers who lived at the same time as Jesus who didn't know Jesus or believe He was God but wrote about Him the way historians today write about famous people. They tell us that Jesus was a real person, that He was killed on a cross, that His friends all believed they saw Him alive, and that they were willing to give their lives for their faith."

"Dad, I've also heard that some people didn't believe Jesus actually died, that He just passed out for a while," added Mom.

Dad thought for a moment and then said, "You know, that is a theory, but it doesn't really work. That Jesus did die on a cross is a fact. His friends all saw Him die and the people who put Him on the cross were very good at their job. They even put a spear in His side to make sure He was really dead and not just faking it or sleeping!" he exclaimed.

"Why did He have to die at all, Daddy?" wondered Joshua. "If He is God, couldn't He just live forever and couldn't He have stopped the soldiers from killing Him?"

Dad paused for a second and then answered, "He could have, yes, but He chose not to. He chose to die for you and for me and for your mom

and sister and everyone else in the world because of His great love for us. That is why today is such a special and joyful celebration for us. When we think about the cross and Jesus' resurrection, we see the clearest, most wonderful picture of God's love for us."

Scripture to Read: 1 Corinthians 15:1–20

Verses to Memorize: 1 Corinthians 15:3–4

Discussion Questions:

1. How do we know that Jesus' tomb was actually empty and that His followers didn't just steal His body and make up a good story?

2. Did Jesus have to die on the cross? If not, why did He die?

3. What do we learn about God's love for us through Jesus' death and resurrection?

4. Why is it important that Jesus rose from the grave on the third day?

7. WHY DOES GOD LET BAD THINGS HAPPEN?

"Breaking news! We're bringing a report from a local gas station, which was just robbed. The culprit left with all the money from the cash register and shot four bystanders upon exiting the establishment. Police are in pursuit of the suspect."

Samantha and Joshua stopped short at the bottom of the stairs, looking in horror at the TV.

"Daddy! Is that true? That gas station is the one by our school!" exclaimed Samantha.

Dad sighed heavily and responded, "Unfortunately, it seems to be true, honey."

"That's just awful," added Mom, switching off the TV.

"Why did it happen?" asked Joshua as the siblings moved into the living room.

"Well," explained Dad, "someone thought that money was more important than human lives, I guess."

"No," protested Joshua, "I mean, why didn't God stop that from happening? If He's so powerful and He loves everyone, why would He let a bad guy shoot those people?"

"Oh, Joshua, come here," Dad said as he drew him into a hug. "I know it sure looks like God wasn't in control of that situation, and your question is one that many people have asked since the beginning

49

of time. Here, let's sit on the couch for a minute." Dad led him to the couch and grabbed Joshua's Bible from the coffee table as he settled in beside Joshua.

Samantha sat on Dad's other side, eager to understand how God could let this awful thing happen.

"Do you know a man in the Bible whose name was Job?" Dad asked.

"No," replied Joshua at the same time Samantha murmured, "I've heard of him."

"This guy had it rough. He was a man who loved God and wanted to please God, but God allowed Job to have all his possessions, health, and most of his family taken away. Job really struggled with how to deal with all that, but in the end, he said in Job 42:2, 'I know that you [God] can do all things; no purpose of yours can be thwarted.' So, in other words, even in the worst of times, God is still powerful and in control," Dad explained.

"Why doesn't He just stop the hurting, then?" Samantha cried.

"We can't begin to understand everything about how God works, but we do know a couple of things that contribute to the hurt in the world. They both have to do with choices. Do you remember the choice that Adam and Eve made at the beginning of the Bible in Genesis 3 when God put them in the Garden of Eden?" Dad questioned.

"Yeah. They chose to disobey God and eat from the tree of the knowledge of good and evil," Samantha responded.

"And what did God say would happen to them if they ate from that tree?" continued Dad.

"They would die," answered Samantha.

"That's right. From that moment they experienced separation from God in spiritual death and then later their bodies died in physical death. Sin's punishment is always death. Through their bad decision, death entered into the world. Here," he said, pushing Joshua's Bible to Samantha. "Read Romans 8:20-22."

Samantha opened to the spot and read, "'For the creation was subjected to frustration, not by its own choice, but by the will of the one who subjected it, in hope that the creation itself will be liberated from its bondage to decay and brought into the freedom and glory of the children of God. We know that the whole creation has been groaning as in the pains of childbirth right up to the present time.'"

"Adam and Eve's sin brought death and sin into the experience of mankind, but it also broke creation so that it would decay and destroy. When we see awful natural disasters like hurricanes and horrible diseases that cause suffering, this is part of the curse on creation itself," explained Dad.

"But what did those four innocent people have to do with Adam and Eve?" Samantha asked.

"That's the other part that has to do with choices. Adam and Eve made their choice, and their choice affects us all. In Ephesians 2:1-3, the Bible tells us that, as a result of sin, our hearts rebel against God too! We want things that God says not to want, and we do things that God says not to do. And just like Adam and Eve, we all make choices that affect others as well. God made us in His image with the ability to make our own choices. That man in the gas station tonight made a very wrong choice to not obey God's Word and those people suffered the consequence of his choice."

"That's wrong. If people are going to make such bad choices, God shouldn't let us make choices. He should just make us do what is good," Joshua retorted.

"That might seem like it would work, but it really wouldn't," Dad responded. "Could you imagine if I told you that, because you chose something at a restaurant that you didn't like, from now on, when we go out to eat, I will choose your food for you? You don't get to make any choices about what to eat or drink. What would you think about that?"

"No fun. I wouldn't like that at all," responded Joshua.

"But then you would never end up with a sandwich you hated like you had at that diner. In fact, you would always only get what was best for you on the menu," countered Dad.

"Still, I would want to look over the menu and choose for myself," said Joshua.

"Of course you would, Joshua. You have the ability to choose and you want to do so. This is a silly little illustration, but it shows why choices matter. God gives us choices and then helps us

to choose to love and follow Him. One choice that God gives us is whether or not to show love to others. We don't always choose right and other people suffer because of our decisions," Dad explained.

"So, creation is broken, we're all dying, and we choose to hurt others. That's just depressing," cried Samantha.

"Hey, chin up, you two. That's not the whole story. That's just the bad news," said Dad while squeezing them both close.

"What's the good news?" asked Samantha, wiping the tears off her cheeks.

"In Isaiah 41:10," Dad began "the Bible says, 'So do not fear, for I am with you; do not be dismayed, for I am your God. I will strengthen you and help you; I will uphold you with my righteous right hand.' Though God allows hard things, He doesn't leave us alone to work it out on our own. He is always holding us up. Another verse your mom and I like to remind each other of is Romans 8:28. It says, 'And we know that in all things God works for the good of those who love him, and have been called according to his purpose.' Even in the toughest times, God has promised to turn all things into good for us. One of those good things is patience. Another is maturity. These things all help us to be like Jesus as we grow during hard times. Speaking of Jesus, flip over to John 11 and read verse 35. It's the shortest verse in the Bible."

"It just says, 'Jesus wept,'" Samantha read with a confused look.

"That's right. His friend had just died. He was grieved by what sin had done to His creation and to His friend. Jesus was weeping along with His friend's sisters. Jesus comforts us, too, when we are sad."

Mom came into the living room, wiping her wet hands on a dish towel. "You know, the thing I have to keep remembering when I'm overwhelmed by the evil and the hurt in this world is that God will one day make a new, perfect heaven and earth."

"Really?" Joshua perked up. "What will it be like?"

"We don't really know all the details about what it will be like. But read in Revelation 21:3 and 4 what we do know, though," answered Mom.

Joshua grabbed his Bible and flipped to the end, "And I heard a loud voice from the throne saying, 'Look! God's dwelling place is now among the people, and he will dwell with them. They will be his people, and God himself will be with them and be their God. He will wipe away every tear from their eyes. There will be no more death or mourning or crying or pain, for the old order of things has passed away.'"

"Did you hear that? No more sin, death, crying, or pain. Everything will be made right again because Jesus, God Himself, became a man and suffered and died on the cross for us to conquer sin and death itself," said Mom.

"There's no easy answer to give people who wonder why God allows so much suffering on earth," Dad said. "After all, Isaiah 55:9 states, 'As the heavens are higher than the earth, so are my ways higher than your ways and my thoughts than your thoughts.' But we do have lots of hope that He comforts us when we suffer, that He can use us to comfort others and bring healing, and that someday He'll eliminate suffering altogether. For now, why don't we pray for everyone involved in this awful situation?"

SCRIPTURE TO READ: PSALM 23

VERSE TO MEMORIZE: PSALM 23:4

DISCUSSION QUESTIONS:

1. What are some bad things that happen in the world as a result of creation being cursed when Adam and Eve sinned?

2. What are some ways your bad decisions have affected others?

3. What good things can come out of bad situations? How can you help others who are going through hard things?

4. What hope do we have for the future?

8. HOW CAN I BE SAVED?

"Hey, Mom! Lexi's here!" shouted Samantha from the front door.

Mom came out of the office, tucking her reading glasses on top of her head. "Hi, Lexi! I'm glad you could come over this afternoon. Do your parents know you're here?"

"They do, Mrs. Lewis," answered Lexi. "My dad just left to pick up my little sister from soccer, but I told him I'd be here for a while. Is that okay?"

"Absolutely! Come in! Come in! I was just about to scrounge up a snack. You girls want to join me?" asked Mom.

"Sure," the girls chimed in unison.

"I'm going to start some popcorn," said Mom as she headed to the kitchen. "Samantha, why don't you wash up some grapes."

After the popcorn popped and the girls had big bowls of it in front of them, Mom sat down at the kitchen table with them. "So, how was school today?" she asked.

Lexi quickly looked down at her bowl, and Samantha glanced between her and her mom with a worried look on her face.

"Oh, I'm sorry," Mom apologized. "Was it a bad day?"

Lexi glanced up. "I got in trouble today at school. One of our teachers caught me on my phone during class. Now I have detention tomorrow and when my parents find out I was on it at school, they'll take my phone away."

"Hmmm. I bet you wish you could take back that decision," replied Mom.

"I do! I should have just followed the rules," confessed Lexi.

"Lexi, what would you say if I told you that I would go serve detention for you tomorrow and you could go free with your afternoon? And what if I let your parents take away my phone instead?" Mom asked.

Lexi giggled. "That would be amazing, I guess. But you can't really do that."

"You're right," admitted Mom, "but wouldn't it be great for you if I could?"

"Yeah, it sure would!"

"Maybe I can't do that for you, but I wonder if you know that Someone did something even more wonderful for you than that," continued Mom.

"Who did what?" asked Lexi, clearly confused.

"Sorry, that was confusing. Let me start over. I know you've been coming to Wednesday night church with Samantha for a while now, and I wondered if you knew that Jesus died for you to pay for your sin," Mom said.

"Well," Lexi shot a look at Samantha, "I hear about it almost every week and Samantha has talked to me some about it, but I guess it doesn't make a whole lot of sense to me."

"Your situation kind of reminded me of it. Do you mind if I share why?" asked Mom.

"No, go ahead," Lexi said and then popped a grape in her mouth.

"Do you remember what sin is?" Mom questioned.

Samantha laughed as Lexi pointed at her full mouth. "Sin is anything we think, say, or do, that goes against who God is and what He's said to do," Samantha chanted the answer she had learned on Wednesday nights at church.

"Right," agreed Mom. "Since God is holy, or perfect, sin is anything we think or say or do that is not perfect. Like lying, stealing, fighting with a sibling, or even . . . not obeying the rules at school. Right?"

"I suppose," inserted Lexi. "But why does God care whether I had my phone out at school or not?"

"He cares because you disobeyed His law by not being obedient to the authority He has put into your life, which is sin, and sin has a huge price tag," explained Mom. "Do you girls remember what Romans 6:23 says? I know you memorized it earlier this year."

"'For the wages of sin is death, but the gift of God is eternal life in Jesus Christ our Lord,'" the girls recited in unison.

"Hey, good job," Mom praised them. "Do you know what wages are?"

"The money you get for doing your job," answered Samantha.

"Right. I go to work, and every two weeks, I receive wages for my work. That's a good thing. Receiving wages for our sin-work is not a good thing, though, because those wages are eternal death, or separation from God forever," explained Mom.

"Forever?" gulped Lexi. "So, not like just a one-time punishment?"

"Forever," confirmed Mom. "Different crimes require different consequences, right? For example, the man who robbed the gas station and shot those people last week should get a much harsher punishment than you got for having your phone in class, right?"

The girls energetically nodded.

"That's because people are worth more than phones. Well, all sin, whether we see it as big or little, is against our perfect, eternal, and all-powerful Creator. Such an offense requires the highest punishment."

Lexi paused and looked into her bowl again as she thought. Then, she muttered, "But that means me, too, because I'm a sinner."

"I know, Lexi. I am too," said Mom, gently touching her arm. "So is Samantha. You've learned Romans 3:23, too, haven't you? All have sinned. Rather than living in obedience to God, we disobey Him and go our own way. But the good news of salvation through Jesus is available for every sinner, to pay our penalty and give us a relationship with God."

"Because Jesus died and rose again, like we talked about on Easter, right Mom?" asked Samantha.

"Exactly right, Samantha," answered Mom. "God is a just Judge and He can't just forget the punishment our sin deserves. But 'God so loved the world that he gave his one and only Son, that whoever believes in him shall not perish but have eternal life.' That's John 3:16, and it means that Jesus, God in the flesh, came from the Father to the earth to live the life we should have and die the death we deserved on the cross to pay the punishment our sin deserved. But He didn't stay dead. He rose and beat sin and death so that we could have 'paid in full' stamped on our account. When we trust in Jesus alone to be our way to a relationship with God and we confess and turn from our sin, He will forgive us, embrace us, help us to live for Him, and allow us to be with Him forever in heaven. It's really neat to put your own name in that verse I just quoted. 'God so loved Lexi that He gave His one and only Son, that if Lexi believes in Him, she shall not perish, but have eternal life.'"

Everyone was quiet for a moment, and then Lexi said, "Mrs. Lewis, I want to live for God and spend forever with God in heaven. I've known for a long time that I'm a sinner, but I guess I thought my sin wasn't so bad that I would really be punished for it. But now I want Jesus to save me from the punishment I deserve and I want to live for Him. How do I do that?"

"Lexi, I'm so happy to hear that," said Mom. "You don't have to do anything but believe that Jesus alone can save you from your sin. We can pray and ask God to forgive you together!"

Lexi, Samantha, and Mom all bowed their heads as Lexi prayed, "Dear God, I know that I don't deserve to be with You in heaven. My sin deserves to be punished and I'm really sorry for all my sin. But I believe that Jesus died for my sin. Thank you for loving me and giving me salvation! Please forgive me and help me to live for you. Amen."

Samantha jumped up and gave Lexi a big hug with tears in her eyes. "Welcome to the family of God, sister!"

Scripture to Read: John 3:13–21

Verse to Memorize: John 3:16

Discussion Questions:

1. Does God love us, even though we sin? Why or why not?

2. Why is sin, even a "small" one, such a big deal?

3. How did Jesus fix our sin problem?

4. What does a person have to do in order to be saved?

9. WHY DON'T MY FRIENDS BELIEVE?

"Yum! This ice cream is so good!" exclaimed Samantha with delight and then quickly caught another drip with her tongue.

"Mmmm," agreed Joshua with his mouth full.

"You know I'll use every excuse I can to go get ice cream with my kids, right?" Dad winked at them over his own ice cream cone.

"I sure do! But I haven't figured out yet how you talked Mommy into letting us come get ice cream," confessed Samantha.

Dad chuckled. "I think she may have been looking forward to a little quiet time to herself. But also, we've been noticing lately how you two are really growing in your understanding of God and the Bible. We're just so happy to see our kids maturing in their relationships with God."

"I have been learning a lot," Samantha commented. "I've been reading my Bible by myself, not just at church, and now that Lexi's a Christian, too, I have someone at school to talk to about what I'm learning. I just wish more of my friends were interested in Jesus."

"Have you talked to them about Him?" asked Dad.

"I've tried. Lexi's been so excited since she got saved that we've both been asking our friends what they think about Jesus."

"And what do they tell you?"

Samantha sighed and took another lick of her ice cream as it dripped down the side of her cone. "Ben says he doesn't want anyone else telling him what to do and that all the rules of church sound dumb to him. Mia says she has her own god and doesn't need mine. Xavier laughed at me and said I was a baby to believe in fairy tales like God. I want to tell people about my faith, but I'm tired of being rejected and made fun of. Why can't they see how great God is?"

"That's tough, kiddo, and you're doing the right thing by telling them about Jesus," encouraged Dad. "Unfortunately, the Bible says—and we see this all around us—that sin has blinded the eyes of unbelievers so they can't see their need for God. Romans 3:11 says, 'There is no one who seeks God.' Left to ourselves, we'd rather not feel bad about our sin or be accountable to a holy God. We'd rather have everything be about us. Remember your brother's last birthday?"

Joshua beamed, but Samantha looked puzzled.

"Uh-huh," she replied.

"Even though it was his special day, you had a hard time because you didn't get any presents or really much attention," explained Dad. "Without God working in our lives, we're all just looking for the party of life to be all about us."

"If that's true, then how did you and Lexi and Mommy and Joshua and I get saved?" asked Samantha.

"God was at work in all of our hearts, taking off our blinders and allowing us to see truth. That's why it's so important to be praying for your friends. Unless God is working in them, they won't see the truth of what you're sharing," said Dad.

"So if they're not going to listen, what do I do? How can I tell when they're ready to listen?" Samantha questioned.

"You can't know, honey, but you can keep loving them and being kind to them even if they're mean to you. Keep showing through your actions as well as your words that Jesus has given you new life and has changed you. When they're ready, they'll listen," supplied Dad.

"And when they're ready to listen?" Samantha asked.

"You watched your mom share her faith with Lexi, didn't you? Ask lots of questions to know what your friends are thinking. Tell them what God's Word says, and then just let God's Word do its work in convicting them of sin and convincing them of who He is."

Samantha nodded slowly and took a big bite of her cone.

Dad noticed that Joshua had stopped eating his ice cream. "What are you thinking so hard about?" he asked Joshua.

"Nothing really. Well, actually, I was just thinking that I've never really tried to tell any of my friends about Jesus. I mean, kids in my class know I go to church and believe the Bible, I guess, and we invited Charlie and his sister to Vacation Bible School last year. But I haven't done anything like Samantha and Lexi. You know, like talking to people in my class," confessed Joshua.

"Why do you think that is," questioned Dad.

Joshua thought a moment and then answered slowly. "I'm scared. I'm not as brave as Samantha and you and Mom. What if someone asks me a question I don't know the answer to?"

"Joshua, I am not brave! I just talk a lot!" inserted Samantha.

"Buddy, you don't have to be like anyone else, and you don't need to have all the answers. Do you know what Jesus has done in your life?" asked Dad.

"Sure! He lived a perfect life and then died in my place and rose from the dead. Because I asked Him to be my Savior, I belong to God now," answered Joshua.

"That's right," Dad assured. "That's your testimony—or firsthand story—of what Jesus has done. That's a great starting point in talking to your friends. You can always tell someone that you don't know the answer to their question but that you can find out. No one knows everything."

"You do," insisted Joshua.

"I'm afraid that's not true," chuckled Dad. "But like you two, I keep asking questions and learning more as I go."

"You know, Joshua, when I wanted to tell Lexi about Jesus, I started praying for her each night before I fell asleep. I think that gave me courage to talk about my faith when I got the chance," said Samantha.

"That's a really great tip, Samantha, and it goes back to what we were just saying about God doing the work to bring people to salvation. Praying for others is a very important first step," added Dad.

"I'll start praying for Charlie, too," Joshua concluded. "And maybe he could come to VBS again this year."

"I think that's a great idea," said Dad. "We can all be praying for Charlie and his whole family. Now, do you suppose we've given Mom enough alone time, or should we stop by the park on our way home?"

"Park!" Samantha and Joshua shouted in unison.

Scripture to Read: 2 Corinthians 5:18–21

Verse to Memorize: 2 Corinthians 5:20

Discussion Questions:

1. Whose job is it to tell others what God has done for us?

2. What do people need to know in order to be saved?

3. How can you show your faith through your words and your actions?

4. Who can you be praying for to have an open heart to hear the gospel?

RESOURCES FOR PARENTS

Here are some resources that you can read to take your journey further!

I. General Apologetics—Defending What We Believe

Hillary Morgan Ferrer, ed., *Mama Bear Apologetics: Empowering Your Kids to Challenge Cultural Lies* (Eugene, OR: Harvest House Publishers, 2019).

Joseph M. Holden, ed., *The Comprehensive Guide to Apologetics* (Eugene, OR: Harvest House Publishers, 2022).

Jason Lisle, *The Ultimate Proof of Creation: Resolving the Origins Debate* (Green Forest, AK: Master Books, 2009).

II. Theology—Explaining the Message of the Bible

Paul Enns, *The Moody Handbook of Theology* (Chicago, IL: Moody Press, 2014).

Norman Geisler, *Systematic Theology: In One Volume* (Minneapolis, MN: Bethany House Publishers, 2011).

John F. MacArthur, ed., *Essential Christian Doctrine: A Handbook on Biblical Truth* (Wheaton, IL: Crossway, 2021).

III. The Doctrine Of God—The Trinity And The Attributes Of God

Matthew Barrett, *None Greater: The Undomesticated Attributes of God* (Grand Rapids, MI: Baker Books, 2019).

Matthew Barrett, *Simply Trinity: The Unmanipulated Father, Son, and Holy Spirit* (Grand Rapids, MI: Baker Books, 2021).

Scott R. Swain, *The Trinity: An Introduction, Short Studies in Systematic Theology* (Wheaton, IL: Crossway, 2020).

IV. The History Of The Bible

John D. Meade and Peter J. Gurry, *Scribes and Scripture: The Amazing Story of How We Got the Bible* (Wheaton, IL: Crossway, 2022).

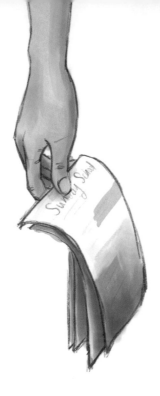

Jason Lisle, *Keeping Faith in an Age of Reason: Refuting Alleged Bible Contradictions* (Green Forest, AK: Master Books, 2017).

James R. White, *Scripture Alone: Exploring The Bible's Accuracy, Authority, and Authenticity* (Minneapolis, MN: Bethany House Publishers, 2004).

V. The Resurrection

Gary R. Habermas and Michael R. Licona, *The Case for the Resurrection of Jesus* (Grand Rapids, MI: Kregel Publications, 2004).

Lee Strobel, *The Case for Christ: A Journalist's Personal Investigation of the Evidence for Jesus* (Grand Rapids, MI: Zondervan Publishing House, 1998).

Michael J. Wilkens and J.P. Moreland, eds., *Jesus Under Fire, Modern Scholarship Reinvents the Historical Jesus* (Grand Rapids, MI: Zondervan Publishing House, 1995).

VI. Science And Faith

William A. Dembski and Sean McDowell, *Understanding Intelligent Design: Everything You Need To Know In Plain Language* (Eugene, OR: Harvest House Publishers, 2008).

Robert Carter, ed., *Evolution's Achilles' Heels* (Powder Springs, GA: Creation Book Publishers, 2014).

Ken Ham, ed., *The New Answers Book,* 4 vols. (Green Forest, AK: Master Books, 2006-2013).

VII. God And Suffering

Randy Alcorn, *If God Is Good: Faith in the Midst of Suffering and Evil* (Colorado Springs, CO: Multnomah Books, 2009).

Nancy Guthrie, ed., *O Love That Will Not Let Me Go: Facing Death with Courageous Confidence in God* (Wheaton, IL: Crossway, 2011).

C.S. Lewis, *The Problem of Pain* (New York, NY: HarperOne, 2015).

VIII. Gender And Sexuality

Hillary Morgan Ferrer and Amy Davison, *Mama Bear Apologetics Guide to Sexuality: Empowering Your Kids to Understand and Live Out God's Design* (Eugene, OR: Harvest House Publishers, 2021).

Carl R. Trueman, *Strange New World: How Thinkers and Activists Redefined Identity and Sparked the Sexual Revolution* (Wheaton, IL: Crossway, 2022).

Rosaria Champagne Butterfield, *The Secret Thoughts of an Unlikely Convert: An English Professor's Journey into Christian Faith* (Pittsburg, PA: Crown & Covenant Publications, 2012).

IX. Tactics For Spiritual Conversations

Natasha Crain, *Talking with Your Kids about God: 30 Conversations Every Parent Must Have* (Grand Rapids, MI: Baker Books, 2017).

Gregory Koukl, *Tactics: A Game Plan for Discussing Your Christian Convictions* (Grand Rapids, MI: Zondervan Publishing House, 2019).

Jay Lucas, *Ask Them Why: How to Help Unbelievers Find the Truth* (Schaumburg, IL: Regular Baptist Press, 2007).

CHRISTIAN
FOCUS

Christian Focus Publications publishes books for adults and children under its four main imprints: Christian Focus, CF4K, Mentor and Christian Heritage. Our books reflect our conviction that God's Word is reliable and Jesus is the way to know Him, and live for ever with Him.

Our children's publication list covers pre-school to early teens. We also publish personal and family devotional titles, biographies and inspirational stories that children will love.

From pre-school board books to teenage apologetics, we have it covered!

Christian Focus Publications Ltd,
Geanies House, Fearn, Ross-shire,
IV20 1TW, Scotland,
United Kingdom.

Find us at our web page: www.christianfocus.com

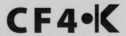